Acknowledgment

Images by CC0 public domain,
these and other photos
can be found at www.pixabay.com

Wikipedia

Male lions sleep 20 hours a day on average.

Lion cubs eyes don't open until about a week after birth.

The lioness goes out and hunts, bring prey
back to the male.

The lioness pregnancy lasts approximately 110 days

Lion range from white to yellow, with various shades in between

The lioness leaves to pride to give birth nearby. They don't return until the cubs are 6-8 weeks old.

Lions sleep and stretch just like our pet cat's do, they are just much bigger.

A lioness has up to 4 cubs at a time, these cubs cuddle and play together as they grow older.

Love the view from up here.

Being cute is so exhausting.

Weaning of the cubs occurs at around 6-7 months.

Male lions are easily recognized by their mane.

I'm ferocious hear my roar.

Male lions weight between 331 and 551 pounds.

Male lions only live up to 15 years, or younger partly due to fight with other males.

Time for a wash.

White lions are not a
subspecies, but a morph
resulting from a genetic
condition.

3 lions in a cuddle pile.

Pride of lions.